Professional Suicide Intervention Techniques for the Mental Health Practitioner

By

Joseph Hayes, MS & Curt Pitton, MA

Chapter 1: "Prologue"

Chapter 2: "Suicidal Intervention Guidance"

Chapter 3: "Suicidal Clients: What to Flag and Reveal in an Assessment"

Chapter 4: "The Manipulative Suicidal Client"

Chapter 5: "Does Everyone Truly Have a Choice?"

Chapter 6: ""Happiness = True Meaning and Purpose"

Chapter 7: "General Facts about Suicide"

Chapter 8: "Age Related Suicide Dynamics"

Chapter 9: "Facts & Fables about Suicide"

Chapter 10: "Profile of Suicide Completer & Suicide Attempter"

Chapter 11: "Completed Suicide High Risk Factors"

Chapter 12: "Warning Signs of Suicide"

Chapter 13: "Shneidman's Model of Suicide"

Chapter 14: "Epilogue"

Chapter 1

Suicide

Going back to the days of being an intern, a suicidal client was a counselor intern's worst fear. Every intern knew that at any moment he could be faced with a client that was going to make an outcry. That's a lot of responsibility to put on an intern as well as an experienced counselor. It is only human to feel the need to offer one's own feelings to assist in a matter. Just think of all the thoughts and emotions currently going through the intern's head. Then, as with the intern, there is the supervisor who must be alerted. This is a pretty compelling situation but with proper training and guidance, the intern can survive and go on to become a licensed counselor.

Suicidal behaviors, outcries, and ideations goes against the basic living organisms drive to live. Every conscious living organism strives to nourish, reproduce, and exist. At least, that's what Darwin's survival of the fittest promotes. Are these drives biological, cultural, or a combination of both? The age old question keeps popping up when attempting to explain behaviors. "Nature VS. Nurture", the human organism is born with reflexes that when stimulated allow it to breath. However, the human mind can be shaped or impacted by the context of it environmental stimuli.

    The American culture generally values the existence of human life. The famous Dr. Jack Kevorkian, was a medical doctor who felt it was his ethical obligation to assist his terminally ill patients with the suicide process. Dr. Kevorkian was seen by many physicians as practicing against the Hippocratic Oath that they are sworn to uphold. After the word got out about his practices, the state intervened and arrested Dr. Kevorkian. Following his arrest, he was found guilty by the courts and sentence to prison for his practices. That's right, prison, for merely helping a terminally ill person commit the act of dying sooner than nature warranted.

Most American Christian religions pronounce the taking of one's life is a sin. Some other country's religions have a different perspective on the taking of one's life. For example, it is known that if a Muslim takes his own life during a martyring act, then the people of that faith tend to praise that act. Muslim belief argues that a person who commits this act has seventy-two virgins awaiting him in the afterlife. Beliefs about suicide are different among cultures.

The American Medical Association has an oath that all physicians must follow. The main point is to do no harm to patients. This belief seems sound and concrete until one gains unique experiences. Working in a nursing home is one that may alter ones view of suicide. Many patients feel that their mind has greatly outlived their physical body due to modern medicine. One author worked in a 24 hour nursing care facility. There he met an elderly lady whom he began to get to know. One day when the counselor asked the lady how she was doing, the lady responded with "I'm just laying here waiting to die". The author possessed only an undergraduate degree and little experience with anyone who didn't care to live. This stunned the author because he did not quite know how to respond. He used logical confrontation, "Now Tessy, you don't really want to die, you're just upset about something". Tessy, the lady, chuckled and replied "You've been reading too many of the psychology books, very few people in my position enjoy life". This puzzled the author so he stood there in silence. Tessy then went on and said "You go get those books and show me where it has any worthwhile reasons for someone like me to live. After all, I'm blind due to diabetes, I've lost my legs to the disease, I have outlived all my family and friends and I just lay up in this room constantly praying for Jesus to come for me as there is no more purpose for my life here on this physical earth anymore". I quit to go back to graduate school not long after this life learning experience. About two months later, I just happened to pick up the newspaper and there was Tessy in the obituary. She had passed in her sleep. I felt a sense of happiness for her as I knew that was what she was waiting on. I will forever be indebted to her for that life lesson on viewing life and death.

Exercises

1. Describe how you would have approached the author's encounter with Tessy. Would you have been different in your thoughts, beliefs, and behaviors?

2. What lesson do you gain from reading about it? Would it be different if you were the one who actually experienced it or can the same value come from reading about it?

Chapter 2

Suicidal Intervention Guidance

To start off with, if you are an intern counselor, social worker or educator please, by all means, seek assistance from your certified trained supervisor immediately if any client who exhibits a direct or indirect manifestation of any self-harming behavior. An experienced supervisor should have the expertise to make a healthy appropriate intervention. Do not be scared and believe you are a bad counselor because you need assistance with a client. We have 25 years of private practice experience and routinely seek consultation from colleagues just to insure clients' gets the best appropriate service from us.

Now, I will go through some important points of suicide screenings with clients who make either an outcry or attempt. The very first session is called an intake. This is an important session as this is a time to gather information, go over the counselor's expectations of and from the client, and begin forming a therapeutic relationship. During the intake, ask the following questions.

1. Have you ever thought of harming yourself or anyone else in the past?

2. Did you attempt these behaviors in the past? If so how, how many times? What was the outcome?

3. Would you attempt these harming behaviors in the future?

4. If these thoughts of self-harming or harming others were to happen in the future, what would you likely do?

5. Do you believe you are stable in the self-harming and other harming area?

When addressing the Informed Consent, Confidential Clauses and Health Insurance

Portability and Accountability Act (HIPAA), inform the client that if he or she makes a suicidal outcry, then you may have to violate confidentiality in order to insure his/her well-being. The client signs an agreement to this violation of confidentiality issue during the intake. Then, explain that suicide and other life threatening behaviors are no laughing matter and will be taken seriously as required by Professional Ethics and Law. Assure the client if he/she is really having those issues then it will be processed in a therapeutic professional manner. It is important to be honest and genuine in the initial encounter with the client so boundaries will be set and known by both client and counselor.

Using the intake to screen the client for potential harming behaviors will give the counselor a partial insight into the client's history, the client's resistance, and attitudes towards help, and the client's present sense of life value. Next, if you begin a counseling relationship and during a session the client makes an outcry of not wanting to live anymore, continue to engage the client in a calm manner. This calmness may help the client feel safe enough to be honest and forthcoming with your intervention questioning. Now there are general lines of questioning one uses to conduct suicidal interventions. There are other avenues out there and more research over the matter being done with different counselors and supervisors that will allow one to grasp the intervention that is best suited for the current client's immediate needs.

Note: Sometimes when counseling adolescents, they want to be helped and will tell a counselor not to tell on them. The counselor needs to divulge any eminent self-harming dangers or other harming dangers. <u>Do not be afraid to notify the parents or responsible party out of fear that the adolescent will not cooperate with further treatment.</u> This still falls under "Duty to Warn" and in my experience the adolescent wants you to inform the appropriate party as it takes the pressure off of them. Oddly enough, many kids want to be told on. One time an adolescent client had stolen a loaded nine millimeter pistol for her boyfriend to shoot another person who was fighting with him. She was going to take it to him Friday night where her boyfriend and this other person were going to meet. The client was asked if it was a real gun and what was her plan. She divulged that she had taken it out of her parents' closet and hid it in-between her mattress at home. She implied it was loaded and she planned on giving it to her boyfriend this evening as it was Friday. She was informed that her parents and possibly the authorities had to be notified. She begged if her parents weren't told she would go and put it back in her parents' closet. She threaten to quit therapy if her parents were told. She was informed there was no choice in the matter and she realized it. Her mother was called at home and was unaware of the situation. The mother went and found the pistol and put it up. She assured the counselor that it wouldn't happen again and she was going to punish her daughter. After getting off the phone, the counselor had to notify the Texas Department of Protection and Regulatory Services because leaving a loaded firearm unsecured in reach of a minor, is considered child endangerment. It was also the counselor's responsibility to call the police department and request a welfare check on the mother's truthfulness of following through with the removal of the pistol and proper placement. The next Friday, the adolescent came back to her therapy appointment and was thankful for what had happened. She expressed relief that she was no longer worried about her boyfriend going to prison because of the intervention, and that he had put her up to stealing the pistol for him. The client then continued treatment as if nothing ever happened.

    It is of the utmost importance to always get identifying information from clients when they communicate with you or your staff. When email was just invented, we remember going to continuing education classes and being told by the instructor to never give or publish our email. Now, we go to many counseling websites and many contact counselor emails are displayed. Things have changed, but the fact that a client could email one a suicide outcry is still a possibility with possible legal liability and obligations.

Chapter 3

Suicidal Clients: What to Flag and Reveal in an Assessment

Now you're a counselor and on your own in private practice. A client that you have been treating for depression comes in for a normal appointment. All signs point to a routine session until the client communicates that he feels like killing himself. This happens in the counseling world, social work, education and medical field. Many factors affect the odds that this will occur in your presence sooner or later. One obvious factor is that the suicide outcries tend to go up during the holiday season.

Suppose you have a client come into treatment and make an outcry. If you have done your intake properly, then you have his identifying information and address. This will be important if the client was to blow up emotionally and vacate your office and presence.

How the counselor reacts upon the client's outcry is important. As a counselor, you should stay calm and in control of emotional overreactions. First, a counselor needs the ability to communicate without avoiding the suicidal issue. It is human nature to not address the issue of death, especially when someone talks of killing one's self. However as a counselor, your empathic response with adequate communicated understanding of the client's feelings will usually validate the client and assist them into a comfort zone of cooperating with your suicide risk assessment.

Second, clarify the client's plan. A reflection question presented would be, "I hear you saying your life isn't worth living anymore and your thought of actually killing yourself concerns me, now what kind of method have you thought of for this action?" This may lead to the client divulging his plan, if he has already thought it through to that point. The intervention information that the counselor needs is: Has the client made a plan? Does he have the actual means of carrying out the plan? These points are very important in helping the counselor in forming an intervention. For example, if a person in jail makes this self-harming statement, a counselor would notify the jail staff to place the client on suicide watch. The staff would insure all objects that could be used are not within the clients reach. Therefore, the client would be highly unlikely to carry out a suicide while under suicide watch. In a mental health facility, suicide watch includes placing the client in "Line of Sight" twenty four hours a day. Knowing the client does not have the means allows the counselor to proceed with attending to the client's feelings and thoughts. This environment would yield a completely different response than a private practice setting environment.

  Third, after positively identifying that the client has a plan and means, gathering more information is essential to a qualitative intervention. The counselor would need to know if the client has ever made a previous outcry. Further, did the client attempt to carry out the last outcry? Also while interacting with the client, see if he contradicts the suicide outcry by talking about future events such as graduating college or attending a family member's future wedding. See if the mind is congruent with the client's outcry of ending his life.

     A counselor should make the decision to seek outside help and to err on the side of caution not on predictability. <u>Interns need to always seek the advice and knowledge of their supervisor.</u> Below we have an unofficial assessment of suicidal potential that we have used as a guide and shared with interns. Having had some clients who did not show any red flags, such as no means or plan, we would have them sign a suicide action plan agreement. Usually this agreement states that if the client has any thoughts of suicide or desire to harm himself, then he agrees to call 911 or the local suicide crisis line. It's even better to get the client's consent to have another responsible adult in the client's life to sign as a witness. That way, the counselor could contact and communicate a concern about the client and see if the client is telling the truth about the safe environment. For example, if the client is dishonest about having any firearms available, then the responsible adult can make sure they get taken up or call the authorities. A 'No Harm" contract is listed at the end of this chapter and may be used or altered to meet the required needs.

12 Important Areas of Assessment of Client Potential Suicide Characteristics

1. Client's admission of suicidal thoughts, intentions, or plans. (The majority of persons that commit suicide communicate their intent, which is why the counselor must listen for indirect and subtle talk of intent.)

2. Duration of time suicidal thoughts have persisted as well frequency and obsession. (Daily, weekly, monthly or just in short episodes)

3. History of thoughts, outcries and if ever engaged thoughts into action. (Client's personal or religious views of suicide.)

4. Communicated Plan (When, where, how?)

   *Exactness of plan (General or precise?)

   *Intensity of success (Gun shot or take pills. Can it be intervened with medical assistance and reversed?)

*Likeliness of successful completion of suicide or can client call for help?

5. Client mood and decision making assessments. (Impulsive, agitated, depressed & loss of control.)

6. Client's recent environmental situations that lead to helplessness and hopelessness. (Loss of relationship, job, divorce, recent death of friend, depravation or separation from family.)

7. Unwilling to sign anti suicide agreement with counselor. (Include willingness to have family member notified about client's condition to insure safe environment free of fire arms, pills and knives.)

8. History of suicidal attempts, family suicidal attempts or friend suicide attempts.

9. No thoughts or mention of any living existence in future occurrences. (Such as being at son's graduation in the future.)

10. Client's current support system. (Does the client identify anyone who cares about his life? Does he or she seek out support? Client's isolation issues. (How long a duration? Is client unwilling to attempt to connect with others? Does client attend church or any social gatherings?)

11. Client's reality stableness. (Does client have psychosis or is he on medication that could interfere with his decision making or reality perception?)

12. Client's Physical Health. (Any terminal illness? Is client's medical condition painful in life? Does medical condition keep him from or hamper him in interacting within a norm of behavioral means with others?)

Suicide Risk Assessment

Additional Specifics

- Screen for history of previous suicide attempts

A) "Share with me any history of suicide activity in your life"

B) "What did you do?"

C) "Why are you still alive?" Explore circumstances of rescue

D) "How are things for your now?"

- Avoid closed-ended "date retrieval" questions – use open-ended format

- A history positive for suicide attempts is a powerful co-relate to eventual death by suicide

- Suicide risk assessment must be a part of any screening or evaluation process regardless of setting

- When to hospitalize a suicidal ideator

- Seek clarification of the goal of the wish to die

    a) Identify the "locus of pain"

    b) Listen for "hopeless metaphors"

    c) Listen for drug use as a "coping strategy"

    d) Seek details on any planning toward this goal

    e) Be aware of access to lethal means

    f) Seek clarification on the emotional reaction to the wish to die

    g) Be aware of "peace & calm" demeanor in person

    h) Seek details on barriers to suicide

- Does person verbalize negative benefits of current therapy?

- Is there impaired judgment due to psychosis?

(Klott, 2012; Hatton & Valente, 1984)

Adolescents Warrant Additional Flags

1. Is the adolescent being bullied by any peers or groups such as the football team?

2. Did an embarrassing rumor or story get posted on the internet?

3. Is the adolescent being harassed because of his political beliefs, religion, race, economic situation or sexual preference?

4. Did one of the adolescent's close friends commit suicide or attempt suicide?

Treatment & Treatment Planning for Suicide Populations

- There are only 2 questions a therapist needs to ask a suicidal person:

    1. "Where do you hurt?"

    2. "How can I help you?"

Everything the therapist does flows from the answer to these two questions.

(Shneidman, Edwin, 1972)

- Problem solving strategies: A behavioral approach

    1. The goal of treatment is stress management, NOT stress elimination

    2. The soul of treatment is the continuous, hope providing relationship between the client and the therapist

    3. The process of treatment is teaching

    (Klott, 2012)

NO HARM CONTRACT

1. I _____, agree not to cause any harm to myself or anyone else during the period _____ to_____.
2. I will try to get enough sleep and eat well.
3. I agree to get rid of anything that could harm me or others (Guns, knives & pills)
4. I agree that if I feel like I might harm myself or someone else, I will immediately call the crisis line at _____ or 911.
5. I have read and or had this contract explained to me.
6. I will go to the emergency room immediately after session if the counselor has instructed me to do so and follow all physicians' orders.

By signing below I am in agreement with all terms and no exceptions.

Client (face to face or phone_____

Date_____

By signing below I am in agreement with all terms and no exceptions.

Counselor (face to face or phone_____
Date_____

If this contract is violated, then the counselor has the right to discharge client and terminate treatment. A referral would then be warranted & given to the client.

(Due to the emergency nature, the counselor has the right to call and verify attendance and if client doesn't self-report attendance and the Hospital doesn't verify, then the counselor will have no other option but to report the client to the police.

Exercises

1. Rearrange the "No Harm" contract to suit your needs in private practice in your local community.

2. Research the local suicide resources in your community and make a list of referrals and contacts.

3. What would you do if a client sent you an email threatening suicide and no one answered his contact phone number?

4. Class divides into groups to discuss the ethics of online/electronic counseling with suicidal clients and what extra procedures need to be taken if conducting this type of therapy?

Notes

Chapter 4

The Manipulative Suicidal Client

There was a Psychiatrist named Dr. B. who was the head of treatment at the Hospitality House, this was a mental health institution that was located in Mount Pleasant, Texas. I was discussing the notion that some suicidal outcry's made by clients seem to be rewarded with attention. He agreed and told me about his paradox psychological suicide intervention. I was very interested as a graduate counseling major.

Dr. B explained that when a client proclaims he wants to harm self or commit suicide; then he as their Psychiatrist would respond with "So you say you want to kill yourself, why don't you just do it?" Dr. B. expressed that he was observing the client's emotional and cognitive responses. He said if they became angry or responded with, "You crazy @#$%, I just might go out and do it. Dr. B.

knew that the logic was intact and congruent if the patient is responding with anger. He stated generally these are the patients that are seeking attention from the outcry. He also went on to say that he would be heavily concerned with the patient that did not respond with anger but instead responded with a calmness, as if it would be no big deal. The client that had no response to his paradoxical intervention was the one more likely to attempt suicide. Now be aware that Dr. B is a medical physician who had done his internship in the field of psychiatry. With that said, clearly, this paradoxical intervention was for information purposes only. Many clients have become treatment wise and utilize crying out suicide for own interest.

Many would ask, "Why would a client purposely make a suicide outcry?" Well for one, the attention itself becomes intrinsically rewarding. The client's worth is all of a sudden praised by others and highlighted. Looking at the ASH studies on group conformity theory, this would explain the clients thinking switching from "no one cares" to "everyone cares about me".

Another reason is to get the attention of a lover who has recently rejected the client. Now that's very powerful to an ex who used to love the client and now they face the guilt that he or she may have been the cause of the client's desire to end their life. Many fall into this manipulation and give into the client's wishes to get back together.

Deep down, clients that use suicide as a manipulation tend to be self-centered. They feel like they are the only ones who suffer in the world. There are usually no feelings about others in the client's life such as mother, father or close friends. The person just usually wants what they want or they threaten to end their life if they don't get it.

This is an obstacle for counselors as even when they sense the client is manipulating the system, they must still attend to the attentive needs of the client as if everyone was seriously going to follow through with the suicide. Not easy even for seasoned counselors, that's why it is good to have resources to assist with the suicidal client. Always take advantage of resources designed to handle such a crisis. In private practice legal liability is a hindering factor when a counselor works with a suicidal client that has a history of such attempts.

Chapter 5

Does Everyone Truly Have a Choice?

Substance abuse disorders with ADHD, Bi Polar disorder, and other disorders have symptoms that we say come from their "Executive Functioning". This means they do not process stimuli in a logical manner. The ADHD clients that we have worked with tend to have very low delayed gratification concepts, if any at all. They tend to be stuck in the here and now. So their sense of rewarding is difficult as they don't demonstrate the ability to wait on rewards. This hampers a person's ability to make sound logical choices. So in essence, the immediate environmental stimuli can influence their choices over delayed logical consequences.

Drug use and abuse similarly cloud a person's judgment and consequent choices and it is no coincidence that addicts, alcoholics, and substance abusers have the highest suicide rate of my group (followed closely by health care professionals, i.e. doctors, dentists, nurses, therapists). It is also surmised that many individuals who commit suicide suffer from something akin to "irresistible impulse" which is an automatic affective response devoid of rational thought. It is this group which is unlikely to leave any kind of "suicide note" because the suicidal act takes place prior to any cognitive awareness of even the possibility of choice. It is unknown, of course, how many people succumb to "irresistible impulse" but several suicide survivors have articulated they were "compelled" to end their lives – it seemed the right thing to do. This groups of individuals is highly unpredictable.

Chapter 6

Happiness = True Meaning and Purpose

A Mental Health Practitioners goal is to have the client buy into the idea that he has the power to be happy. A therapist may assist his suicidal client into seeking happiness by finding true meaning and purpose. Happiness is a product of living one's true meaning and purpose in life. This is of the highest importance in lifestyle change.

People who live a mistaken meaning are only going through the motions in life. They are living by habit not life. They go to work, eat some pizza, watch late night television and get up the next day to do the same. Finding one's true meaning is similar to the pursuit of happiness. If you are not enjoying life then look at the area that seems to be keeping you from obtaining a true meaning and purpose. <u>Life is like a video game</u>. There are lots of different games to meet a variety of different peoples' needs. Now that you found the game you like, you put a quarter in and start playing it. You become excited by behaviors of moving a lever or hitting buttons. If I walk up behind the machine and pull the plug from the wall, you can still move the lever and push the buttons (going through the motions) but there is no longer any satisfaction. By pulling the plug I took away all meaning and purpose behind the behavior of moving the lever and pushing the buttons. Life is very similar in that if you're just going through the motions (moving levers, pushing buttons) then you are not going to be happy.

    Many people claim things are important in their happiness, but tend to devote little time to these values. Client after client will claim that their children or family are important and make them happy. Have them analyze the amount of time spent with their children/family over a seven day period. Talk about defensiveness, most people become aware that they spend more time on the computer, than interacting with their family and children. You will even get the argument that they spend quality time with their family and children and that is what counts. Always challenge that logic with if quality time was food and you gave you just a small amount of the highest quality food once a week, you would bet you would still starve to death or show signs of needing food. So that argument is an excuse because family and children need quantity time as well. Remember those of you who don't believe this, there will be a day later in your life that you will wish you had spent more quantity time with them. This time is usually when they have grown up, they will contact you only for quality time. As they will put many other things in front of family life and interaction, just like they were taught to do by your modeling behavior. A good movie that relates to this is "Click" by Adam Sandler.

There are other factors that are biological that come into play in achieving happiness. That is why they prescribe antidepressants and other medications. People may have a hormonal imbalance or sugar diabetes that can cause mood disturbances. Be sure to rule out all medical causes by letting your client know that if they try and try and still are not able to become happy, then a medical checkup would be warranted to rule out medical conditions.

Chapter 7

General Facts about Suicide

80% of persons who experience suicidal ideation communicate their plans to family members, friends, authority figures (e.g., physicians, pastors) or telephone programs (Hewett, 1980).

Suicide seldom occurs without warning (Shneidman, 1985).

Almost all human beings think about the possibility of suicide at one time or another (Hewett, 1980).

Note: There is a profound difference between the person who says they wish they were dead and the person who says they have a plan to die (Shneidman, 1985).

The more the person has thought about suicide, the more likely they have a plan for suicide, and plans indicate that any and all suicidal remarks must be taken seriously (Shneidman, 1985).

Suicide attempts are 3 times more common among females than among males (Garland & Zigler, 1993).

Suicide completions are 5 times higher for adolescent and adult males as for adolescent and adult females (Garland & Zigler, 1993).

1 in 13 people in the U.S. have attempted suicide (National Center for Injury Prevention & Control, 2000).

12 out of every 100,000 actually succeed in committing suicide (Blau, 1996).

20% of high school students in the U.S. have experienced suicidal ideation (National Center for Injury Prevention & Control, 2000).

Recently divorced or separated adults are more likely to commit suicide (Stark & Wasserman, 1993).

There is a higher rate of suicide (attempted and completed) by 3 to 1 in homosexual versus heterosexual teens (Cato & Sanetto, 2003; Savin-Williams & Ream, 2003).

Copycat Suicide:

When the news media present sensational coverage of a particular mode of suicide, the number of people who attempt and complete suicide using that method markedly increases (Ashton & Donnan, 1981).

Individuals who have already been thinking about taking their own life may become more likely to after viewing a television program or reading a newspaper article in which a person carries out a similar suicide plan (Samaritans, 1998).

Chapter 8

Age Related Suicide Dynamics

CHILD/ADOLESCENT SUICIDE: Child & Adolescent suicide are attempts to achieve a temporary escape from a stressful personal problem (Blau, 1996).

Many children & adolescents who attempt suicide believe that death is a pleasurable experience for most people who die (Gothelf et. al., 1998).

In child suicide (individuals below the age of 12) suspected gross physical, sexual, and/or emotional abuse of a prolonged nature, although even one act of severe physical or sexual abuse can induce a suicide attempt (Klott, 2012).

ADULT SUICIDE:

Suicidal adults typically think of death, even when deserved, as painful and unpleasant (Gothelf et.al., 1998).

ELDERLY/GERIATRIC SUICIDE:

Elderly suicides (i.e., individuals over 70 yrs. of age) contain a theme that is seldom present in those of younger individuals – the idea that one is a burden to others (Foster, 2003).

More elderly woman (75 yrs.+) attempt suicide than men, but elderly men are 3-5 times more likely to complete suicide (Foster, 2003).

Elderly white males (75 yrs.+) are more likely to commit suicide than any other group (National Center for Health Statistics, 1997).

Chapter 9

FACTS & FABLES ABOUT SUICIDE

I. People who talk about suicide rarely commit suicide. **FALSE**

   Eight out of 10 persons who commit suicide talk about it first.

II. Suicide happens without warning. **FALSE**

   Suicidal persons give any clues and warnings regarding suicidal intentions.

III. Suicidal people are fully intent on dying. **FALSE**

   Usually there is a "cry for help", though often given in "code".

IV. Once a person in suicidal, he/she is suicidal forever. **FALSE**

   Most people who are suicidal are only suicidal for a limited time period.

V. Improvement during a suicidal crisis means that the suicidal risk is over. **FALSE**

Most suicides occur within about 3 months following the beginning of improvement, when the person has the energy to put his morbid thoughts and feelings into effect.

VI. Suicide strikes more among the rich – or, conversely it occurs more frequently among the poor. **FALSE**

Suicide is represented proportionately among all levels of society.

VII. Suicide is inherited or "runs in the family". **FALSE**

Suicide does not run in families. However, if there is a history of successful suicide, a person is at higher risk of suicide or attempted suicide (the same is true if the individual has had friends and/or lovers who have committed suicide – hence, it's not familial per se).

VIII. All suicidal individuals are mentally ill, and suicide is the act of a psychotic person.

FALSE

Though depressed, angry, frustrated and extremely unhappy, suicidal individuals are rarely mentally ill (and mentally ill people rarely commit suicide).

Shneidman, E.S. & Farberow, N.L. (1961)

Chapter 10

Profile of the Suicide Completer

- Male

- Caucasian

- Age 15-55 & 65+

- Living alone & unemployed

- Suffering from depressive or anxiety disorder & substance abuse disorder with the purpose of self-medicating

- Not in therapy

- Extreme issues of fatalism, despair and self-devaluation

- No intent communication

- Visited a primary care professional within six months of suicide

Profile of the Suicide Attempter

- Female
- Caucasian
- Age 20-40
- Social isolation
- Lack of vocational/occupational definition
- Substance abuse/dependency
- Emotional regulation challenges
- Axis I with co-occurring Axis II concerns
- Use of reversible means – focus on "operant" goals

(Klott, J. 2002)

Chapter 11

Completed Suicide High Risk Factors

- Behavior problems, such as aggression

- Family history of psychiatric disorders

- Family history of attempted & completed suicides

- Prolonged unemployment

- Social isolation

- Poor physical health (Kaplan & Sandock, 1991)

- Previous suicide attempts

- Family history of drug/alcohol abuse

- Some triggering stressful event

    a) Usually a disciplinary crisis with parents

    b) Some ejection or humiliation, such as breaking up with a boyfriend/girlfriend, or failing in a valued activity.

    c) Marked rejection by peers (Young & Bradley, 1998)

- An altered mental state

    a) Sense of hopelessness, helplessness, or haplessness

    b) Reduced inhibitions from alcohol/drug consumptions

    c) Rage

- An opportunity

    a) A loaded gun laying around the house

    b) A bottle of sleeping pills in the parents' medicine cabinet

(Shaffer, Garland, Gould, Fisher & Trautman, 1998; Swedo et. al., 1991)

Chapter 12

Warning Signs of Suicide

(1) Giving away prized possessions

(2) Giving away all of one's possessions

(3) Marked change in eating and/or sleeping habits.

(4) Marked depression (severe reduction in brain serotonin levels)

(5) Aggressive/hostile actions and/or verbalizations

(6) Passive, indifferent attitude and/or behavior

(7) Fear of separation

(8) Abrupt changes in personality

(9) Sudden mood swings

(10) Decreased interest in loved activities

(11) Marked negative and/or cynical attitude

(12) Inability to focus and concentrate

(13) Marked hopelessness

(14) Marked listlessness

(15) Alcohol and/or drug abuse

(16) Obsession with death

(17) Significant expressions of self-devaluation and self-hate

(18) Refusal to seek help

(19) Marked dysphoria

(20) No capacity for futuristic thinking

(21) Expressed apathy toward all aspects of life

(22) Previous suicidal ideation and/or gesturing

(23) Suicide notes, letters, art, poetry

(24) Anhedonia

(25) Morbid, shame-based preoccupation with the past

(26) Verbalized comments of despair and/or fatalism

Klott, J. (2012)

Chapter 13

Shneidman's Model of Suicide

<u>Triggering Process:</u>

(1) Inimicality, or an unsettled life pattern in which one acts against one's best interests

(2) Perturbation, or an increased psychological disturbance in the person's life

(3) Constriction, which appears in "tunnel vision" and "either/or" thinking, leading to a narrowing range of perception, opinions, and options that occur to the person's mind

(4) Cessation of resolving the unbearable pain of disturbance and isolation by simply stopping or being out of it

Ten Common Characteristics of Suicide

Situational Aspects

(1) The common stimulus in suicide is unendurable pain

(2) The common stressor in suicide is frustrated psychological needs

Cognitive Aspects

(3) The common purpose of suicide is to seek a solution

(4) The common goal of suicide is cessation of consciousness

Affective Aspects

(5) The common emotions in suicide are hopelessness, helplessness, haplessness (being ill-fated or unlucky)

(6) The common internal attitude toward suicide is ambivalence

Cognitive Aspect

> **(7)** The common cognitive state in suicide is <u>constriction</u>

Relational Aspects

> **(8)** The common interpersonal act in suicide is <u>communication of intention</u>
>
> **(9)** The common action in suicide is <u>egression</u>

Serial Aspect

> **(10)** The common consistency in suicide is with <u>lifelong coping patterns</u>

(Shneidman, E.S., 1985)

Ten Practical Measures for Helping Suicidal Persons

(1) Stimulus (unendurable pain): Reduce the pain

(2) Stressor (frustrated needs): Fill the frustrated needs

(3) Purpose (to seek a solution): Provide a viable answer

(4) Goal (cessation of consciousness): Indicate/find alternatives

(5) Emotion (hopelessness): Provide hope

(6) Internal Attitude (ambivalence): Play for time

(7) Cognitive State (constriction): Increase/find the options

(8) Interpersonal Act (communication of intent): Listen to the cry; involve others

(9) Action (egression): Block the exit

(10) Consistency (with lifelong patterns): Invoke previous patterns of successful coping

(Shneidman, E.S., 1985)

Chapter 14

Epilogue

Over sixty-five years ago, the psychiatrist Karl Menninger, in his book, "*Man, Against Himself*", noted that suicide, regardless of what form it took, was "homicide directed against oneself." Thus, suicide is "self-murder" and _ Menninger also noted that in his 40 years of psychiatric work with patients, that anyone capable of suicide, was equally capable of homicide. It should be noted that since roughly 1960 approximately one quarter to one third of all suicides have been homicide/suicides. In the past 50 years murder by police homicide/suicide, adolescent suicide, and child suicide have all increased by over 150%.

As Freud pointed out over 100 years ago, suicide, or at the very least suicidal ruminations typically results from chronic frustrations of "EROS" (the life instinct) and its replacement with 'Thanatos' (the death instinct). For Freud, chronic frustrations of the life instinct results from a lack of love, acceptance, validation, an respect on the part of the suicidal victims parents, family, friends, lovers, community, and/or significant other. Though suicide is still regarded as a flaw or weakness by most members of American society, and has a horrible stigma attached to it, it should be noted that if conditions are right, anyone and perhaps everyone, might succumb to it. There are few American families that have not been touched by suicide and even fewer individuals who have never experienced a suicidal thought or desire at some time during their life. It is, however, a tragedy that can be avoided if one knows what signs and symptoms to look for. It is hope that the perusal of this book will assist one in not only a better understanding of suicide, but in a better diagnosis, intervention, and treatment of it. That, at least, is the hope of both of its authors. The rest is up to you.

Definitions

Consumer – a past or present recipient of mental health services.

Suicide attempt survivors – people who have experience with suicidal thinking and behaviors including individuals who have survived a suicide attempt.

Survivors – family members, significant others, acquaintances, or providers of health services who have lost a loved one or client due to suicide.

The term suicide is often used broadly to include thinking about suicide, self-harming behaviors, suicide attempts, and deaths by suicide. It is important to be clear about what aspect of suicide is being discussed.

Death by suicide – death from a self-inflicted act (e.g., injury, poisoning, or suffocation where there is evidence that the act was intentional).

Deliberate self-harm (DSH) – intentional self-injurious behavior where there is no evidence of intent to die.

• DSH includes various methods by which individuals injure themselves, such as self-laceration, self-battering, taking overdoses, or exhibiting deliberate recklessness.

Suicidal communications – direct or indirect expressions of suicide ideation, expressed orally or through writing, artwork, or other means.

Building Bridges: Suicide Prevention Dialogue with Consumers and Survivors

Suicide attempt – a non-fatal, self-inflicted act (e.g., injury, poisoning, or suffocation) with explicit or inferred intent to die.

• Death does not occur in an attempt for one of the following reasons: the act was not lethal; the person was rescued or thwarted; or the individual changed his or her mind. A suicide attempt may or may not result in injuries.

Suicide ideation – thoughts of harming or killing oneself.

• People who have suicide ideation may or may not form the intent to do themselves harm. They may or may not have a plan. Ideation may be transient or ruminative, active or passive, acute or ongoing.

Efforts to prevent suicide may be categorized in the following ways.

Prevention – interventions designed to stop suicide attempts or completions from occurring by focusing efforts on at-risk individuals, environmental safeguards, reducing the availability of lethal methods, and systemic reform.

Intervention, support, or treatment – the care of suicidal people by peers, loved ones, certified peer specialists, consumer-operated services, licensed mental health caregivers, health care providers, and other caregivers with individually tailored strategies designed to support, empower, respect, and change the behavior, mood, and/or environment of individuals, and help them identify and satisfy their needs without engaging in self-destructive behaviors.

Post-intervention – actions taken after a suicide has occurred largely to help survivors such as family, friends, and co-workers cope with the loss of a loved one.

Warm lines – confidential non-crisis telephone support lines answered by trained consumers who offer support, hope, strength, understanding, and a willingness to listen.

• The operators of warm lines span all the stages of recovery from mental illnesses.

(Definitions were used from the public domain source. http://www.samhsa.gov/shin. Or, please call SAMHSA's Health Information Network at 1-877-SAMHSA-7 (1-877- 726-4727) (English or Espanol).)

References

Ashton J. & Donnan, S. "Suicide by burning as an epidemic phenomenon: An analysis of 82 deaths and inquests in England and Wales in 1978-1979." *Psychological Medicine*. 1981. 11, 735-739.

Blau, G & Gullotte, T (Eds). "Adolescent depression and suicide." *Adolescent dysfunctional behavior: causes, interventions, and prevention*. Newbury Park, California: Sage, 1996. 187-205.

Cato, J. & Canetto, S. "Attitudes and beliefs about suicidal behavior." Roles, Sex. 2003. 49, 497-505.

Foster, T. "Suicide note themes and suicide prevention." *International Journal of Psychiatry and Medicine*. 2003. 33,323-331.

Garland, A.F., & Zigler, E. "Adolescent suicide prevention: Current research and social policy implications." *American Psychologist*. 1993. 48, 169-182.

Gothelf, D., Apter, A., Brand-Gothelf, A., Ofer, N., Ofek, H., Tyano, S., & Pfeffer, C. "Death concepts in suicidal adolescents." *Journal of the American Academy of Child & Adolescent Psychiatry*. 1998. 37, 1279-1286.

Hatton, C.L. & Valente, S.M. *Suicide: Assessment and intervention (2nd ed)*. Norwalk CT: Appleton-Century-Crofts, 1984.

Hewett, J. *After Suicide*. Philadelphia: Westminster Press. 1980.

Kaplan, H. & Sadock, B. *Sypnosis of Psychiatry (6th ed)*. Baltimore, MD: Williams & Williams, 1991.

Klott, J. "Suicide & Self-Mutilation: Stopping the Pain." Dallas, TX, 2014. CMI Education Institute Seminar.

"National Center for Health Statistics." *Vital Statistics of the United States*. Washington, D.C.: U.S. Government Printing Office, 1997.

"National Center for Injury Prevention and Control (NCIPC)." *Fact book for the year 2000*.

Washington, D.C.: U.S. Government Printing Office, 2000.

Samaritans. *Medical guidelines on portrayals of suicide*. 16 February 2001. <http://www.mentalhelp.net/samaritans/medreport.htm.>.

Savin-Williams, R. & Ream, G. "Suicide attmepts amoung sexual-minority male youth." *Journal of Clinical Child & Adolescent Psychology*. 2003. 32, 509-522.

Shaffer, D., Garland, A., Gould, M., Fisher, P., & Trautman, P. "Preventing teenage suicide: A critical review." *Journal of the American Academy of Child & Adolescent Psychiatry*. 1988. 27, 675-687.

Shneidman, E.S. *Definition of Suicide*. New York: John Wiley & Sons, 1985.

Stack, S. & Wasserman, L. "Marital status, alcohol consumption, and suicide: an analysis of national data." *Journal of Marriage & the Family*. 1993. 55, 1018-1024.

Swedo, S. C., Rettew, D.C., Kuppenheimer, M., Lum, D., Dolan, J., & Goldberger, E. "Can adolescent suicide attempters be distinguished from at-risk adolescents?" *Pediatrics*. 1991. 88 620-629.

Young, M. & Bradley, M. "Social-withdrawal, self-efficacy, happiness and popularity in introverted and extroverte adolescents." *Canadian Journal of School Psychology*. 1998. 14, 21-35.

This material/publication is produced by Joseph D. Hayes MS and Curt Pitton MA. No commercial copying or use without one of the author's written authorization. Visit http://www.counselorjoe.com to obtain permission through email. This material is the sole opinion, experience or perceptions of the counselors performing in their fields. Given the nature of the clients, The Authors express "There are no guarantees of success in using any of these techniques with actual clients" These techniques are for learning purposes and should not be used by anyone who is not supervised by appropriate licensed Mental Health Practitioners or who is not licensed by the state to perform counseling. Only Licensed Professionals with appropriate experience should attempt and utilize these techniques at his or her own risk.

Printed in Great
Britain
by Amazon